ESCAPING A SINKING SHIP

BY EMILY ROSE OACHS

The Child's World®
childsworld.com

Published by The Child's World®
1980 Lookout Drive • Mankato, MN 56003-1705
800-599-READ • www.childsworld.com

Photographs ©: Everett Historical/Shutterstock Images, cover, 1, 11, 14; Art Media Heritage Images/Newscom, 5; akg-images/Newscom, 6, 16, 24; Ann Ronan Picture Library Heritage Images/Newscom, 8; USS Arizona Collection/AZ 517 Box 17 Folder 19/courtesy of University of Arizona Libraries, Special Collections, 18; US Navy/National Archives, 20; iStockphoto, 22; AP Images, 28

ISBN 9781503825291
LCCN 2017959687

Printed in the United States of America
PA02377

TABLE OF CONTENTS

FAST FACTS

- For thousands of years, ships made of wooden **hulls** ruled the seas. The first metal-hulled ships appeared in the 1840s. At first, they were made of iron, followed by steel in the early 1880s.
- Metal ships were safer than those made of wood. They were stronger, more durable, and more difficult to damage than wooden ships.
- Between 1880 and 1930, steam-powered ocean liners carried tens of millions of passengers across the Atlantic Ocean. Many were immigrants searching for a new life. Some were wealthy travelers and businesspeople, crossing the ocean in luxury.
- Records show that in ancient times, people used air-filled animal skins for flotation. In the mid-1800s, early modern life jackets were made of cork. Later life jackets relied on air, foam, and lightweight wood from kapok and balsa trees for **buoyancy**.
- Although the invention of the lifeboat came in 1790, it took until 1914 for regulations to require that all ships carry enough lifeboats for every person on board.

Ships usually sink because of war or weather, or because they were poorly built. ▶

- Nobody knows exactly how many ships have sunk throughout history. But experts estimate that more than 3 million shipwrecks lie on Earth's ocean floor.

Chapter 1

THE RMS *TITANIC*, 1912

The night of April 14, 1912, was cold and moonless on the northern Atlantic Ocean. The RMS *Titanic* steamed through the still, glassy waters. A multitude of stars shone bright and clear overhead.

Speedy and luxurious, the *Titanic* was the largest ship in the world. People claimed it was unsinkable. Approximately 2,200 people sailed aboard the ship on its maiden voyage.

Around 11:30 p.m., 17-year-old Jack Thayer was preparing for bed. He and his parents were first-class passengers on the *Titanic*. The Thayers had boarded the ship in Southampton, England, on April 10.

Jack had just said good night to his parents. Suddenly, he felt the ship sway and heard the rumble of the ship's engines stop.

◂ **The *Titanic* could carry up to 3,547 people.**

Jack and his father went up to the deck to investigate and discovered pieces of ice littering the deck. Earlier that day, they had heard reports of nearby icebergs. The *Titanic* had struck one, a crew member told them.

Jack and his father did not think the situation was serious at first. Then, they ran into Thomas Andrews, the *Titanic*'s designer. He gave them grim news. Badly damaged by the iceberg, the *Titanic* would not survive the night.

Jack and his father went back to their cabin, where they and Jack's mother put on life jackets as instructed by passing crew. When they returned to the deck, the Thayers encountered Milton Long, a friend they had met on board.

At first, the *Titanic*'s passengers did not realize their lives were in danger. But soon, they felt the ship **listing** to one side. Water had started to fill the ship through holes gashed in its side from the iceberg. The ship was sinking. As the reality settled in, the passengers grew panicked. Everyone on board was headed straight into the frigid Atlantic Ocean.

All of a sudden, Jack and Milton lost Jack's parents in the sea of frantic passengers. Together, the friends searched for Jack's parents as the ship continued to list steeply to the side.

◀ **The iceberg that the *Titanic* struck was nearly 100 feet (30 m) tall.**

They listened to a band that was playing cheerful tunes, each member wearing a life jacket. Crowds of people fought to get into the lifeboats, while bright distress rockets burst overhead.

More than 2,000 people were on board the *Titanic*. Yet the ship was equipped with only 20 lifeboats, enough for approximately half of the passengers and crew. Still, crew members prepared, loaded, and lowered the lifeboats to save those they could.

At 2:15 a.m. on the morning of April 15, the ship was sinking fast. Water was flooding the ship's deck. Crew members had released all of the ship's lifeboats into the ocean, although many of them had not been completely filled. For the hundreds of passengers still on board, few options for escape remained.

Jack and Milton had to jump into the freezing water. "Go ahead," Jack told his friend. "I'll be with you in a minute." Milton leaped over the ship's railing and slid down the ship's side. He disappeared into the Atlantic, never to be seen again.

A few seconds later, Jack followed. "The cold was terrific," Jack later remembered. "The shock of the water took the breath out of my lungs." At 28 degrees Fahrenheit (–2 degrees C), the water was below freezing.

It took nearly 3 years to build the *Titanic*. It took barely 3 hours for it to sink into the ocean. ▶

Jack fought to swim through the icy water. His lungs cried for air. Finally, he surfaced approximately 40 feet (12 m) away from the ship.

Jack looked at the ship that towered above him. Trailing down the center of the ship were four massive funnels, or smokestacks.

TITANIC TIMELINE

- **11:40 p.m.** - A lookout spots the iceberg. The *Titanic* does not have time to change its course. The right side of the ship is struck.
- **12:05 a.m.** - Lifeboats are uncovered and prepped for passengers and crew.
- **12:20 a.m.** - Lifeboats begin boarding women and children. The distress call sent from the *Titanic* is received by the *Carpathia*.
- **12:45 a.m.** - The first lifeboat is lowered to safety, with less than half of the boat's capacity filled.
- **2:05 a.m.** - The last lifeboat is lowered. There are more than 1,500 people left to die on the ship.
- **2:17 a.m.** - The last radio message is sent from the *Titanic*.
- **2:20 a.m.** - The last of the *Titanic* sinks into the sea.
- **4:00 a.m.** - The *Carpathia* arrives to save the remaining survivors.

The second funnel had started to fall. It appeared to be headed straight for Jack. He watched in fear as it slammed into the ocean just a few yards away. It had missed Jack, but its powerful suction dragged him underwater.

Jack struggled to the surface, desperate for air. Then, he felt something floating overhead—an overturned **collapsible** lifeboat. A few other men already clung to the boat's bottom. Jack, soaking wet and freezing, climbed up with them.

Jack watched as the *Titanic* disappeared into the ocean. A chorus of wails soon rose from people floating in the icy water. Many more people climbed onto Jack's boat. Gradually, the overturned lifeboat started to sink into the ocean. The survivors needed rescue soon. They couldn't survive the cold much longer.

Hours later, Jack spotted lights from the RMS *Carpathia*. The ship had heard the *Titanic*'s distress calls. The *Carpathia* had come to rescue the survivors of the *Titanic*.

Jack was among the last of the approximately 700 people to be rescued. On board the *Carpathia*, Jack spotted his mother immediately. Their ordeal was over. Jack and his mother had survived the sinking of the *Titanic*, but his father was never found.

Chapter 2

THE RMS *LUSITANIA*, 1915

The sky was bright and the sea was still on the afternoon of May 7, 1915. The British liner RMS *Lusitania* was nearing the end of its voyage across the Atlantic Ocean. It had left New York six days earlier, on May 1. Now, it was sailing along Ireland's coast, a day away from its destination of Liverpool, England.

By May 1915, World War I had been going on for 9 months. On one side were the Central Powers: Austria-Hungary, Germany, and Turkey. They fought against the Allies, which included Britain, France, Italy, and Russia.

The war had turned parts of Europe's countryside into bloody battlefields. Even the seas were not safe. Germany had made it clear that it was willing to **torpedo** British ships sailing through war-zone waters.

◂ **The *Lusitania* weighed 32,000 tons (29,000 metric tons).**

▲ **There were nearly 2,000 people on board the *Lusitania*.**

Some of the *Lusitania*'s passengers had come to the decks to admire the beautiful views of Ireland. Yet hidden beneath the ocean's deep blue waters, enemy German **U-boats** lurked.

Seventeen-year-old Alice Lines was in her cabin with baby Audrey Pearl and five-year-old Stuart Pearl. Alice was one of two nannies traveling with American naval surgeon Warren Pearl, his wife Amy, and their four young children. Alice was feeding Audrey when she heard a loud bang. Immediately, the nanny launched into action. Using a shawl, she tied Audrey to her chest.

Alice and the children raced out of the cabin. They needed to get onto the deck to the lifeboats. A second torpedo struck the ship as they ran up the stairs.

The boat was sinking fast. It leaned hard to one side. Alice, Stuart, and Audrey safely reached the upper deck. They fought their way to the lifeboats, where sailors grabbed Stuart from Alice's grasp and placed him in a lifeboat.

Alice attempted to follow with baby Audrey, but the sailors stopped her. There was no more room on the boat, they told her.

The lifeboat began to lower toward the water. Desperate, Alice leaped over the railing and into the freezing cold water. She was not even wearing a life jacket.

Her long hair spread out around her in the water. A sailor in Stuart's lifeboat reached down and grabbed Alice's hair, pulling her and Audrey into the lifeboat. Alice and the children were safe.

From the lifeboat, Alice watched as the *Lusitania* quickly disappeared below the water's surface. Just 18 minutes had passed since the first torpedo struck.

Nearly 1,200 people died in the attack. Alice, Audrey, and Stuart were among the 800 survivors. Later, Audrey and Stuart were reunited with their parents. But their two sisters and nanny Greta were never found.

Chapter 3

THE USS *ARIZONA*, 1941

December 7, 1941, started out as a normal Sunday morning at Pearl Harbor, an American naval military base in Hawaii. Some crew members ate breakfast in their ship's mess hall, while others prepared for church.

Then, around 7:55 a.m., the nearly 100 ships stationed at Pearl Harbor—along with the other ships of the Pacific Fleet—received an urgent telegraph message. "AIR RAID ON PEARL HARBOR X THIS IS NOT A DRILL." Alarms began to sound, alerting crew members to report to the decks. Japanese planes were attacking the base.

World War II had been raging overseas between the Axis and Allied powers for two years. Japan, Germany, and Italy made up the Axis powers.

◄ The USS *Arizona* was built in 1915.

▲ **Wreckage from the USS *Arizona* still leaks oil into the ocean to this day.**

The Allied powers included Great Britain, France, and the Soviet Union. Since the war's start in 1939, the United States had managed to stay out of the fighting.

Donald Stratton was a crew member on board the USS *Arizona*, a battleship stationed in Pearl Harbor. He ran to his station, a control tower armed with **anti-aircraft guns**.

From there, he and others tried to shoot down the Japanese planes that flew high overhead.

Almost 15 minutes into the attack, a bomb hit the USS *Arizona* and struck the ship's **ammunition** stores. One million pounds (450,000 kg) of gunpowder exploded, blasting the ship out of the water and splitting it in half. A ball of fire consumed the ship.

With flames raging on deck below the tower, Donald and five other men were trapped. Donald's clothes and skin begin to burn, and he could feel the intense heat of the fire below through the soles of his shoes. Then, he and other crew members spotted a sailor named Joe George on board the *Vestal*, a maintenance ship tied to the *Arizona*.

The Japanese attack had already badly harmed the *Vestal*. Still on *Vestal*'s deck, Joe noticed six crew members in a tower on the *Arizona*. They waved to him frantically as fire surrounded them. The *Arizona* was sinking fast. They were desperate for help.

Joe's commanding officer called for him to cut all ties between the two ships. The officer worried that the sinking *Arizona* would drag the *Vestal* down with it. Joe ignored the order. With the *Arizona* sinking and burning, Joe knew that refusing the officer's order was the only chance the men had at survival. Joe tossed a line over to the *Arizona*, and the *Arizona* crew members caught and secured it.

▲ **The USS *Arizona* memorial was built in 1962.**

One by one the men left the USS *Arizona*. They had suffered terrible burns. Still, they pulled themselves across 75 feet (23 m) of line, from their tower to the *Vestal*'s deck.

Donald struggled to cross. The fire burned his hands badly. Below, blazing flames leaped from slicks of oil on the water.

From above, Japanese bullets whizzed past. Donald looked and saw Joe watching him from the *Vestal.*

"C'mon, kid!" Joe called out. "You can do it!"

Donald and the other men made it across safely. All had burns covering much of their bodies. The flames had charred their skin.

Approximately 2,400 Americans, mostly soldiers, died in the attack on Pearl Harbor. Of those, nearly 1,200 had been on board the USS *Arizona.* Donald was among the ship's mere 335 survivors. Joe, the man who rescued Donald and the other sailors, survived the attack, too.

PEARL HARBOR DAMAGE

The USS *Arizona* was not the only ship to face devastation on December 7, 1941. Three torpedoes quickly struck the USS *Oklahoma* in the first few minutes of the attack. The ship sank within ten minutes, nearly completely flipping over in the water. Beside the *Arizona,* two bombs hit the *Vestal.* The second dropped through the *Vestal*'s deck and smashed a hole through its hull. The *Arizona*'s explosion had also blasted *Vestal* crew members into the water below.

Chapter 4

THE *WILHELM GUSTLOFF*, 1945

In January 1945, 10-year-old Horst Woit lived in the German province of East Prussia with his mother, Meta. Germany and its allies were struggling as World War II neared its end. Enemy Soviet forces entered Horst's city. They brought ruthless destruction to East Prussia as they murdered Germans, set towns ablaze, and stole from shops and homes.

Fearing for their safety, Horst and his mother decided to flee to Gotenhafen, Poland. As they packed up their belongings, Horst found a jackknife that belonged to his uncle. He tucked it into his pocket, stealing it.

In Gotenhafen's harbor, the *Wilhelm Gustloff* waited. It would carry **refugees** like Horst and Meta to safety in Kiel, Germany. The *Wilhelm Gustloff* had originally been built as a cruise ship. It was meant to carry only 1,888 passengers and crew members.

◂ **Adolf Hitler was present when the *Wilhelm Gustloff* first launched on May 5, 1937.**

But many people wanted to seek safety from the invading Soviet army. Officials packed the ship with about 10,500 fleeing refugees. Passengers crowded together to sleep in the ship's ballroom and its emptied swimming pool.

The *Wilhelm Gustloff* set sail on January 30, 1945. Nobody on board knew that a Soviet submarine followed unseen beneath the waves. A few hours into the *Wilhelm Gustloff*'s journey, around 9 p.m., the first Soviet torpedo struck.

In their cabin, Horst's mother shook him awake. He woke to hear the thunderous bangs of the second and third torpedoes.

NOT ENOUGH SAFETY EQUIPMENT

The *Wilhelm Gustloff* was not equipped with enough safety equipment for all 10,500 people on the ship. There were not even enough life jackets for all passengers. Twenty-two lifeboats lined the ship's decks. But as the ship sank, it tilted deeply to the side. This meant half the lifeboats, high in the air, were unusable. On the other side, crew members realized with dismay that some of the lifeboats were frozen to the deck. Of the 22 lifeboats, crew members loaded and lowered fewer than ten.

The corridors were crowded with people. The ship was already tilting hard to one side. Horst and Meta sprinted for the stairs. They reached the top safely, but other passengers were not so lucky. Throughout the ship, the stampede of terrified passengers crushed others running for the upper decks.

On deck, the winter night was freezing, hovering around 0 degrees F (–18 degrees C). But luck was with Horst and Meta. Crew members quickly helped them into a lifeboat. Then, the boat slowly lowered into the choppy waters of the Baltic Sea.

The *Wilhelm Gustloff* was sinking quickly. Horst's lifeboat needed to move away from the ship before it went under, or else the *Wilhelm Gustloff* would drag the small lifeboat down with it. But something got in the way.

"The ropes are frozen to the lifeboat!" a man's voice cried out. "We cannot get away from the ship. Who's got a knife?"

Approximately 70 people filled the lifeboat, many of them children. Nobody responded. Nobody had a knife.

Then Horst remembered his uncle's knife. He carefully pulled the stolen knife from his pocket and passed it toward the man. The man was able to cut through the frozen ropes.

The lifeboat broke free from the ship. Two men quickly rowed it away. At 10 years old, Horst and his stolen knife had saved the lives of himself, his mother, and 68 other people.

Wilhelm Gustloff

By the next morning, Horst, Meta, and the other survivors of the *Wilhelm Gustloff* were safely on board German rescue ships. But their numbers were few. Only approximately 1,200 people survived, while an estimated 9,000 died in the attack. No other marine disaster had ever lost so many passengers.

THINK ABOUT IT

- People in the military have a duty to follow their superiors' orders. Yet Joe George disobeyed his officer's orders to save the lives of Donald Stratton and other men on the USS *Arizona*. Do you think he was right to do this? Why or why not?
- What steps could officials have taken before the *Wilhelm Gustloff* set sail to make the ship safer for its passengers?
- How have new advances in technology helped oceans become safer for ships?

◄ **The number of people who died on the *Wilhelm Gustloff* was more than five times the amount that died on the *Titanic*.**

GLOSSARY

ammunition (am-you-NISH-uhn): Ammunition is the explosive materials that are fired from rockets, guns, and bombs. The USS *Arizona's* store of ammunition exploded when struck by a Japanese bomb.

anti-aircraft guns (ant-i-AYR-kraft GUNS): Anti-aircraft guns are weapons of war that are used to shoot planes overhead. Donald Stratton shot at Japanese enemy planes using anti-aircraft guns.

buoyancy (BOY-ans-ee): Buoyancy is the ability of something to float in water. The buoyancy of life jackets helps people float while they wait for rescue in the water.

collapsible (kuh-LAP-suh-bel): Collapsible means that something is able to be folded up. Jack Thayer held tight to the bottom of the overturned, collapsible lifeboat as he watched the *Titanic* sink.

hulls (HULZ): Hulls are the watertight bodies of ships. Ships made of wooden hulls were used for travel for thousands of years.

listing (LIST-ing): Listing is leaning or tilting to the side. After striking an iceberg, the *Titanic* began taking on water and listing to one side.

refugees (re-fyoo-JEEZ): Refugees are people who must flee their homes to seek safety from war and violence. Horst, his mother, and many other refugees crowded on board the *Wilhelm Gustloff* to flee the dangers of war.

torpedo (tor-PEE-doh): To torpedo is to attack a ship by launching from a submarine an underwater bomb called a torpedo. During World War I, Germany threatened to torpedo any British ships sailing through waters in the war zone.

U-boats (YOU-bohts): U-boats are German submarines. Sailing beneath the ocean's surface, German U-boats waited to attack passing enemy ships.

TO LEARN MORE

Books

Demuth, Patricia Brennan. *What Was Pearl Harbor?* New York, NY: Penguin Books, 2013.

Fredeen, Charles. *Eyewitness to the Sinking of the* Lusitania. Mankato, MN: The Child's World, 2018.

Sabol, Stephanie. *What Was the* Titanic? New York, NY: Penguin Books, 2018.

Web Sites

Visit our Web site for links about escaping a sinking ship:
childsworld.com/links

Note to Parents, Teachers, and Librarians: We routinely verify our Web links to make sure they are safe and active sites. So encourage your readers to check them out!

SELECTED BIBLIOGRAPHY

Adams, Simon. *World War II.* London, England: DK Publishing, 2014. Print.

Archibald, Gracie, and Jack Thayer. Titanic*: A Survivor's Story.* Chicago, IL: Academy Chicago Publishers, 2010. Print.

King, Greg, and Penny Wilson. Lusitania*: Triumph, Tragedy, and the End of the Edwardian Age.* New York, NY: St. Martin's Press, 2015. Print.

INDEX

ABOUT THE AUTHOR

Emily Rose Oachs graduated as a member of Phi Beta Kappa from the University of Minnesota with a degree in communication studies. She has authored more than 50 nonfiction books for children and young adults on topics ranging from natural disasters and biomes to geography and history. She lives and writes in Los Angeles.